by I

Series editor: Roger Phillips

Elm Tree Books in association with the British Museum
(Natural History)

INTRODUCTION

This book illustrates 80 of the 200 or so species of birds which regularly breed in or visit the British Isles. Other species are mentioned in the text where necessary for identification purposes.

Residents and migrants

Many species can be seen in Britain all the year round, and are referred to as residents. However, others only visit us at certain times of year. Summer visitors come here to breed, and move south to southern Europe and Africa in winter, while winter visitors are birds which have bred farther north and come to Britain in winter. Passage migrants are birds which pass through in spring or autumn on their journeys between summer and winter quarters. It should be pointed out that even many apparent residents may migrate, with some British breeders moving south in winter while others move in from the north. The status of each species is explained in the text.

Bird-watching

Many of the species included in this book are common garden visitors, so seeing them is an easy matter; the provision of a bird table will help attract them. Others will be encountered in the course of countryside walks. Generally, a short walk with frequent stops of a few minutes or so is to be preferred to covering a lot of ground at too great a pace. Birds will often reveal themselves to an observer who sits quietly, when they would keep out of sight of a walker. A pair of binoculars is an invaluable aid; 7× or 8× magnification is sufficient in most situations. Calls are an important aid to identification, but cannot easily be conveyed in words. A recording of bird calls is a help, and still better is a walk with an expert.

Blackbird in midwinter

Birds and the law

Most species of British birds are protected by law, and it should be the cardinal rule of all bird-watchers to put the birds' interests first. Nesting birds are particularly vulnerable to disturbance, and any sign of alarm calls or agitation during the breeding season should be taken as a signal to move away. Photography of nesting birds, of which this book contains many excellent examples, is best left to the experts; special licences are in any case required for such activities.

Clubs and Societies

If you are developing an interest in birds and bird-watching you will benefit greatly from meeting others with similar enthusiasms. Most areas have their local natural history societies or bird clubs, and there are also three important national organisations in Britain:

The Royal Society for the Protection of Birds (The Lodge, Sandy, Bedfordshire, SG19 2DL) furthers its aims by owning and managing nature reserves, and in various other ways. It runs a network of local Members' Groups which hold interesting programmes of meetings and publishes *Birds*, a readable and lavishly illustrated magazine. The RSPB also runs a lively junior branch called the Young Ornithologists Club.

The British Trust for Ornithology (Beech Grove, Tring, Hertfordshire, HP23 5NR) exists to coordinate the observations of amateurs so that information of national importance can be gathered. It runs ongoing surveys, such as the Common Birds Census, the Birds of Estuaries Survey, and the Ringing Scheme, and also carries out one-off surveys into topics of special concern. It publishes two journals, *Bird Study* and *Ringing and Migration* as well as the quarterly *BTO News*.

The British Ornithologists' Union is the senior ornithological body in the country, and publishes the important scientific journal *Ibis*.

Great Crested Grebe

Great Crested Grebe

Length 19 inches (48 cm)

Podiceps cristatus is unmistakable in breeding plumage, when it has a striking crest and ear-tufts. In winter, the ear-tufts are lost and the face is mainly white, but the slender neck and dagger-shaped bill distinguish it. During the last century its head adornments almost brought about its extinction in Britain, for they were in much demand for the millinery trade. With protection, its numbers have returned to healthy levels, and it is now a common sight on lakes, reservoirs and gravel pits.

In early spring, a visit to such places may be rewarded with a display of the Great Crested Grebe's elaborate and beautiful courtship rituals. The nest is a floating platform of water weeds, and when leaving its 4 eggs, the parent bird pulls nest material over them to conceal them. The chicks have an elegant pattern of longitudinal stripes, and make a charming sight when riding on the parent's back, a common habit.

4

Great Crested Grebe nest and eggs

Cormorants nesting on rock stack

Cormorant

Length 36 inches (91 cm)

The dark plumage and characteristic body shape of *Phalacrocorax carbo* distinguish it from all other seabirds except its smaller and scarcer relative the Shag (*P. aristotelis*) which, however, has an all dark face in adult plumage. It is often to be seen standing on a rock or buoy with wings outstretched to dry. In flight, the neck is stretched out with the head held fairly high, and parties often fly in chain formation.

Cormorants are skilled fishers, diving for fish from the surface of the water and pursuing them with great agility under water. They have been persecuted by fishermen in some areas for their supposed depletion of salmon and trout stocks, though these form only a small proportion of their diet. In China and Japan, by contrast, fishermen train Cormorants to fish for them! Cormorants breed in colonies, building their large nests of sticks and vegetation on coastal rocks or in trees by large inland waters. 3 or 4 eggs are laid.

Cormorant

Grey Heron and young

Grey Heron

Length 36 inches (91 cm)

With its grey and white plumage, long neck and legs and long black crest, the Heron, *Ardea cinerea*, is easily identified. In the air it is equally distinctive, flying with head and neck drawn back, legs extending behind, and with slow flaps of the broad rounded wings. The call is a harsh, resounding 'fraank'.

Herons hunt by standing motionless in shallow water waiting for unwary fish to pass by, when the neck is extended with lightning speed to stab or seize the victim. Other creatures such as frogs, voles or young birds are also taken. Breeding in colonies called heronries, the birds usually site their large stick nests in trees, sometimes cliffs or reedbeds. 3 to 5 pale blue eggs are laid, and the quaint-looking young are fed on regurgitated food. Heron numbers fluctuate, being adversely affected by prolonged freeze-ups which deprive them of open waters for fishing.

Grey Heron

Mute Swan nest and eggs

Mute Swan

Length 60 inches (152 cm)

Familiar and well-loved, the Mute Swan, *Cygnus olor*, can be confused with the Whooper and Bewick's Swans (*C. cygnus* and *C. bewickii*) which visit us from the Arctic in winter. The Mute Swan's orange bill with a black knob at the base distinguishes it from its northern relatives, which have black and yellow, unknobbed bills. In flight, the Mute Swan's wings produce a loud throbbing beat, another identifying feature.

Mute Swans feed on a variety of water plants, dipping their long necks under water to reach them, or grazing by the water's edge. In winter they may feed in large flocks on lakes, rivers or estuaries, but during the breeding season they are strongly territorial. The nest itself – a huge mound of vegetation – is fiercely defended even against man. The downy grey cygnets take some 18 weeks to attain the power of flight, but a further 4 years to assume the pure white adult plumage.

Mute Swan

Canada Goose nest and eggs

Canada Goose

Length 36–40 inches (91–102 cm)

Although an introduced species, *Branta canadensis* is probably our most familiar wild goose, since it is resident and relatively tame. Several other species visit us in winter, but must be sought in more remote areas, usually near the coast. It is also our largest goose; this, and its striking plumage pattern make it easy to identify.

As its name suggests, it was originally a North American species, introduced here during the 17th century to ornament the lakes of parks and estates. It has now spread throughout England and into parts of Scotland, and breeds on reservoirs and gravel pits. The nest is made of the goose's own down, and is sited for preference on a small island as a precaution against predators. The gander spends much time guarding his sitting mate prior to the hatching of 5 or 6 downy yellow goslings.

Canada Goose

Male Mallard

Mallard

Length 23 inches (58 cm)

Glossy green head, chestnut breast and grey flanks make the drake Mallard, *Anas platyrhynchos*, easy to recognise. The female resembles those of several other ducks, but may be known by the violet-blue patch of feathers in the wing. Like other ducks, the male goes into 'eclipse' when moulting, and then resembles the female. The flight is fast and strong, with rapid wing beats. Its usual call is the familiar 'quack'.

The Mallard is a 'dabbling' duck, that is, one that obtains food by up-ending in the water, rather than actually diving. Most of the food is plant matter of various kinds. It is the ancestor of most domestic ducks, and often becomes very tame in town parks or canals, though birds living on marshes or estuaries are much more wary. It nests in water-side vegetation or even tree hollows, from which the ducklings, usually 9–12 in number, have to tumble to the ground. They take over 7 weeks to achieve the power of flight.

Female Mallard and ducklings

Male Tufted Duck

Tufted Duck
Length 17 inches (43 cm)
Smartly attired in black and white, with a long drooping crest at the back of his head, the male Tufted Duck, *Aythya fuligula*, could be confused only with the much scarcer Scaup (*A. marila*), a winter visitor, distinguished by its pale grey back. The female Tufted Duck is less distinctive, its plumage a duller, brownish version of the male's, but it does have a short crest, visible at close range. In flight, both sexes show a broad white wing bar.

In contrast to the Mallard, the Tufted Duck dives for its food, which is predominantly animal. Molluscs are a particular favourite. It is our commonest diving duck, its numbers having increased greatly this century. It is an example of a bird which has actually benefited from man's encroachment on the countryside, because this has been accompanied by the development of numerous gravel pit lakes and reservoirs. Tufted Ducks conceal their nests in water-side vegetation and lay 8–12 eggs from which hatch a brood of dark brown ducklings.

Female Tufted Duck incubating

Sparrowhawk nest and eggs

Sparrowhawk

Length 12 inches (30 cm) male, 15 inches (38 cm) female

The larger size of the female, a general feature of birds of prey, is particularly marked in this species, *Accipiter nisus*. Sparrowhawks are often confused with Kestrels, though they are very different birds. The Sparrowhawk's greyish upperparts and barred underparts distinguish it when perched, while in flight its short rounded wings give it quite a different outline from the Kestrel; also it never hovers.

The Sparrowhawk feeds almost entirely on small birds captured in flight. Its hunting techniques make maximum use of cover; a frequent ploy is to fly swiftly low along a hedge, and then dash suddenly over to the other side to surprise an unwary victim. Because of this, it is less often seen than the Kestrel. Sparrowhawks nest in woodland, favouring conifers where available. The stick nest is placed high in a tree, and 4 to 6 eggs are usually laid. The young fledge after about 4 weeks, and are fed by the parents for a further 2 or 3 weeks until competent at hunting for themselves.

Sparrowhawk

Buzzard

Buzzard

Length 20–22 inches (51–56 cm)

The Buzzard (*Buteo buteo*) in flight is sometimes mistaken for the larger and rarer Golden Eagle (*Aquila chrysaetos*), but can be distinguished by its shorter, blunter head outline and proportionately shorter wings. Moreover, the Golden Eagle is virtually confined to Scotland, whereas the Buzzard is also common in the west of England and Wales. Perched on a tree or telegraph post by the roadside, a Buzzard at rest adopts an upright, hunched posture. The markings of the underparts show great individual variation.

Buzzards are most numerous in well-wooded hilly or mountainous areas. Rabbits are an important item of diet, but the Buzzard is not averse to carrion such as road casualties. The bird illustrated has captured a wood mouse. The bulky stick nest is placed in a tree or rock ledge, and a territory generally includes 2 or 3 old nests which are refurbished and used in rotation. 2 or 3 eggs are laid, and the young are at first clad in white down. They take 6 or 7 weeks to fledge.

Buzzard feeding on woodmouse

Kestrel eggs

Kestrel

Length 13–14 inches (33–36 cm)

Hovering as it seeks for prey on the ground, the Kestrel, *Falco tinnunculus*, is now a familiar sight along our motorways. This habit alone is almost sufficient to identify it, but the rufous upperparts, streaked underparts and pointed wings distinguish it from the Sparrowhawk, our other common bird of prey. The male is distinguished from the female by his grey head and tail and less heavily barred back.

Although popularly associated with major roads, the Kestrel can hunt successfully in a wide variety of open country habitats and even in towns. Small rodents and insects form much of the diet, though in many areas birds such as Starlings and House Sparrows are important prey, especially during the breeding season. Kestrels make no nest, but find a hollow in a tree, cliff or building, or the old nest of a Crow, in which to lay their 3 to 6 eggs. The young fledge in about 4 weeks, and then disperse widely, a small proportion even moving to continental Europe.

Male Kestrel and young

Kestrel juvenile

Peregrine and young

Peregrine Falcon
Length 15–19 inches (38–48 cm)
Falco peregrinus is usually seen in the air; this master of the skies can be identified by its pointed wings, short tail, blunt head profile and powerful flight. When perched it is known by the mottled grey upperparts and black 'moustaches'.

Once threatened by the effects of pesticides in the environment, the Peregrine has shown a welcome recovery since stricter controls were enforced. Nevertheless, a trip to the wilder parts of Britain is necessary to see it, as it is a bird of mountains and coastal cliffs. It is famed for its hunting technique – a spectacularly swift dive or 'stoop' to strike down another bird with a single blow. Prey up to the size of grouse are regularly taken, and it is much favoured by falconers. It nests on cliff ledges or in old Ravens' nests, laying 3 or 4 eggs. After fledging, the family may sometimes be seen in the air together making mock stoops at one another.

Peregrine with prey

Female Pheasant on nest

Pheasant

Length 30–35 inches (76–89 cm)

Resplendent male or camouflaged female, the Pheasant, *Phasianus colchicus*, is almost too familiar to need description. Young birds are sometimes confused with Partridges, but can always be told by their longer tails.

Familiarity comes not only from seeing Pheasants alive in the countryside, but also from the rows of dead ones in poulterers' shops around Christmas. Its tasty flesh was no doubt the reason for its introduction from eastern Europe in the early Middle Ages, and it continues to be a popular sporting bird today. Many are incubated and reared artificially to be released on large estates, but Pheasants also breed wild. Early in spring, males duel with one another, to the accompaniment of loud crowing, aiming to accumulate a harem of several females. Clutches of up to 15 eggs are laid in ground scrapes well-hidden by brambles or other vegetation. The chicks are mobile soon after hatching, and can fly in a mere two weeks, long before they have finished growing.

26

Male Pheasant

Moorhen eggs in old Magpie nest

Moorhen

Length 13 inches (33 cm)

A dark grey and brown bird, deep-bodied, with a bright red bill base and long greenish legs and toes, the Moorhen, *Gallinula chloropus*, is unmistakable out in the open. However, it spends much time amongst shady water-side vegetation; the continual flicking of its white under-tail-coverts, or the white line along its flanks, may be the first thing to catch the eye. These marks also identify the duller coloured immatures.

Almost any small pond or stream may harbour Moorhens, and they are sometimes seen feeding out in open fields some distance from water, though they always return there if alarmed. Feeding on a mixed animal and vegetable diet, Moorhens are strongly territorial and quarrelsome. They may breed 2 or 3 times a year, siting the nest amongst water plants or sometimes in bushes or the old nest of another bird. The example illustrated is in an old Magpie's nest. Moorhen chicks have black down contrasting with bright blue bare crowns.

28

Moorhen incubating

Coot chick

Coot
Length 15 inches (38 cm)
Fulica atra is an all-black water bird with a white bill and white shield on the forehead. Although related to the Moorhen, it is much more aquatic, possessing lobed toes to aid swimming, a striking feature when it is seen out of the water. These are noisy birds, with pinging, metallic calls.

Coots obtain much of their diet of water-plants by diving, and require fairly deep water in their habitat. Hence they are found on large stretches of water such as gravel pits and reservoirs, as well as some smaller ponds and rivers. The nest of dead water plants is placed among reeds or flags growing in shallow water. 4 to 8 eggs are laid, buff with fine black spots, and the chicks which hatch from them have a bizarre appearance, well-illustrated in the photograph above. Immatures slightly resemble those of the Moorhen, but are known by their whitish underparts.

Coot

Oystercatcher nest and eggs

Oystercatcher

Length 17 inches (43 cm)

Black-and-white plumage, long vermilion bill, and incessant piping calls make the Oystercatcher, *Haematopus ostralegus*, one of the easiest waders to identify. Strongly gregarious, it is often seen flying along the shore in groups in skein formation, showing striking white wing bars.

Although oysters are rarely taken, the bird is a mollusc-specialist, and has special adaptations for dealing with these hard-shelled prey. The strong, chisel-tipped bill can be used to hammer open prey such as cockles or mussels, or to stab through a partly open shell to sever the adductor muscle. Individual Oystercatchers specialise in one or other technique. Some birds also feed inland on earthworms and other prey. The nest is a simple scrape in sand, shingle or bare earth inland, and 2 to 4 eggs are laid. The beautifully camouflaged chicks leave the nest after a day or two, and can fly at about 5 weeks. Most Oystercatchers migrate south as far as Spain in winter, being replaced by birds from Iceland and Scandinavia.

Oystercatcher at nest

Avocet chicks

Avocet

Length 17 inches (43 cm)

Recurvirostra avosetta, a supremely graceful black and white wader, with its upturned bill and long blue legs, has become familiar as the symbol of the Royal Society for the Protection of Birds. It is equally distinctive in flight, its legs extended behind, and frequent ringing calls of 'klewit'.

It is an apt symbol, for its re-establishment as a British breeding bird after a long absence was a major success for the RSPB. It still breeds in good numbers on reserves managed by the Society on the east coast. Nesting is colonial, the birds laying their 2 to 4 eggs in scrapes lined with plant scraps close to the water. The chicks have camouflaged down at first, but even from an early age show the upturned bills as seen in the illustration above. Ringing has shown that there is considerable interchange between British and continental Avocet populations. Most British birds and some continental ones winter in this country, both on the east coast, and at several sites in the south-west.

Avocet

Ringed Plover chick

Ringed Plover
Length 6 inches (15 cm)
On the coast, the face and breast pattern of the Ringed Plover, *Charadrius hiaticula*, and its short stubby bill, are sufficient for identification. By fresh water, care must be taken to distinguish it from the rarer Little Ringed Plover (*C. dubius*), known by its all-dark bill and legs and yellow eye-ring. In flight, the Ringed Plover shows a white wing bar, lacking in the Little Ringed, and its disyllabic call differs from the latter's sharp single pipe.

Shingle banks along the coast are the typical breeding habitat, and the nest is a simple scrape with little in the way of lining. 4 eggs are laid, their colour and markings blending perfectly with their surroundings; indeed, they are so well camouflaged that there is great danger of holiday-makers treading on them unawares near popular seaside resorts. The chicks are also camouflaged, their black and white collars helping to break up their outline. Ringed Plovers from southern Britain are mainly resident, but those breeding further north may migrate to France or Spain in winter.

Ringed Plover on beach

Lapwing in flight

Lapwing

Length 12 inches (30 cm)

Pied plumage with green-glossed back, long crest and the characteristic 'peewit' call identify this familiar farmland Plover, *Vanellus vanellus*. In flight it is unmistakable, with broad rounded black and white wings.

The Lapwing's tumbling display flight, strange squealing song and humming wing beats are evocative of early spring. The nest is a scrape on bare earth or amongst crops or grass, containing 4 beautifully marked eggs. The pattern of the downy chicks echoes the adult plumage, but is nevertheless excellent camouflage. The Lapwing feeds on earthworms, grubs and various insects obtained from the ground or amongst grass roots. Its foraging tactics, alternating short runs with pauses to watch for prey is characteristic of Plovers. During winter, Lapwings are often seen in large flocks on farmland, but are quick to move when hard weather threatens, travelling to Ireland or southern Europe in search of milder conditions. Occasional individuals wander as far as North America!

Lapwing settling on eggs

Dunlin feeding on mudflats

Dunlin

Length 7 inches (18 cm)

In breeding plumage, *Calidris alpina* is a handsome little wader, with a tortoiseshell mottled back, and black belly. However, winter and juvenile plumages are drab. Confusion is then possible with a number of other small waders, but the Dunlin has a fairly long down-curved bill, a white wing bar and a dark centre to the rump.

As a British breeding bird, the Dunlin is mainly confined to moorland and some coastal habitats, where its presence is revealed by the trilling song given in display flight. 4 eggs are laid in a scrape in a grass tussock, and the chicks are patterned above in black and brown with white spangling. In winter it feeds on mudflats in flocks which may number several thousands, many of them visitors from the Arctic and Scandinavia. Flocks in flight manoeuvre in unison, appearing from a distance like animated smoke. On the mud, they move busily, pecking and probing constantly in search of small crustaceans, molluscs and worms.

Dunlin

Snipe nest and eggs

Snipe

Length 10½ inches (17 cm)

Often first seen as it rises unexpectedly from a pool or ditch, the hoarse call and zigzag flight of the Snipe, *Gallinago gallinago*, permit instant recognition. The Snipe's plumage is excellent camouflage, and it often escapes detection until the last minute. Seen properly, the striped head and back and the extremely long, straight bill are characteristic. Confusion is possible only with the less common Jack Snipe, (*Lymnocryptes minimus*), a winter visitor.

Snipe breed in water meadows, marshes and wet moorland. The presence of breeding birds is revealed by the extraordinary display flight in which a strange 'bleating' sound is produced by air rushing through specially modified tail feathers as the bird dives. 4 eggs are laid in a well-hidden scrape, and the chicks are a rich chocolate with black and white markings. Short when first hatched, the bills quickly grow to enable them to become expert probers for earthworms and grubs.

Snipe feeding

Curlew nest and eggs

Curlew

Length 20–23 inches (51–58 cm)

Far-carrying calls of 'courlee' permit identification of the Curlew, *Numenius arquata*, when it is still a speck in the distance. Closer to, its size (our largest wader) and very long down-curved bill, make it unmistakable. In flight it shows a white rump and back, but lacks any wing bar. The only species resembling it is the smaller and less numerous Whimbrei, (*N. phaeopus*), which is distinguished by a striped head pattern and relatively shorter bill.

Moorlands are the typical nesting habitat, but Curlews are breeding increasingly on farmland in lowland parts of England, usually in cereal fields or silage grass. In the display flight, the male circles round his territory uttering a song in which repeated 'courlee' calls merge into a long bubbling trill. The 4 eggs are laid in a deep scrape, and the chicks can fly after 5 to 6 weeks. Outside the breeding season, Curlews are largely coastal birds, feeding on small crabs or probing for worms, molluscs, etc.

44

Curlew and chick

Redshank chick

Redshank
Length 11 inches (28 cm)
Rising with piercing alarm calls from a salting creek, the Redshank, *Tringa totanus*, displays striking white wing patches and a white rump which are immediately diagnostic. Seen on the ground, the combination of mottled brown plumage and orange-red legs distinguish it. The only species which can sometimes be mistaken for it is the much scarcer Spotted Redshank (*T. erythropus*), a passage migrant. This is quite distinct in its all-black breeding plumage, but at other times of year can resemble the Redshank quite closely. However, it is a greyer, longer-legged bird than the Redshank, and the leg colour is a darker red.

Redshanks breed in a variety of marshy habitats, both inland and on the coast. The 4 eggs are laid in a scrape concealed in a tussock or other vegetation. After the breeding season, Redshanks move to coastal mudflats, some continuing south as far as Spain.

Redshank

Male Turnstone incubating

Turnstone
Length 9 inches (23 cm)
Handsomely clad in breeding plumage, the tortoiseshell back, white crown and black breast make the Turnstone, *Arenaria interpres*, instantly recognisable. It is duller in winter and juvenile plumages, but can still be recognised by the short orange or yellow legs and sharply pointed bill. In flight it shows a complicated pattern of black and white on wings, back and tail unlike any other wader.

Its behaviour is also a guide to recognition, for it is aptly named. It does indeed turn over small stones, seaweed and driftwood in order to reveal prey, of which the small crustaceans known as sandhoppers are the most numerous. Unusually among waders, it will also eat carrion in the form of beach-washed dead birds and mammals. It occurs on coasts of all types, though preferring rocky or stony shores and breakwaters. Although it may have bred in Scotland on rare occasions, this is really an Arctic breeder, seen here chiefly as a spring and autumn passage migrant.

Turnstones

Black-headed Gull nest and eggs

Black-headed Gull

Length 14–15 inches (36–38 cm)

Strictly speaking dark brown rather than black, the dark head distinguishes *Larus ridibundus* in breeding plumage from all but a few rare visitors. For much of the year though, the head is white, with just a small black spot behind the eye, and the red bill and legs are the best distinction from other small gulls. In flight a broad white patch along the leading edge of the wing is a diagnostic feature. Immature birds have a dark diagonal band across the wing coverts.

Black-headed Gulls nest colonially, some on coastal marshes or dunes, but many by inland waters, sewage farms, etc. The nest is a simple platform of dead plant material, and 2 or 3 eggs are normally laid. Although gull chicks are well-developed when hatched, they stay on or near the nest for a considerable time, and are fed by their parents. This is necessary in a colony, because young which wander too far from the nest are liable to be savagely attacked by other gulls!

50

Black-headed Gull

Herring Gull in flight

Herring Gull

Length 22–26 inches (56–66 cm)

Larger than the Black-headed, the combination of a pale grey back with yellow and red bill distinguishes *Larus argentatus* from other British gulls. The legs are usually pinkish. Immature birds have a mottled brownish-grey plumage, and change gradually to the adult grey and white over their first 3 years. The typical call is a clear, repeated 'klew-klew-klew-klew', perhaps one of the most characteristic sounds of the seaside.

Herring Gulls breed in colonies, laying 3 eggs as a rule in the nest of plant debris. The chicks are fed by regurgitation, and the red spot on the parents' bill is an important signal stimulating their begging responses. Cliffs and rocky hillsides by the sea are the typical breeding habitat, but sometimes Herring Gulls nest on rooftops, often causing a public nuisance in the process. The problem is basically a man-made one, however, for this species has increased greatly as a result of such human creations as refuse tips and reservoirs, where gulls often roost in huge numbers.

Herring Gull

Common Tern chick and egg about to hatch

Common Tern

Length 14 inches (36 cm)

Though related to gulls, terns are easily distinguished by their slim build, black cap, long forked tail and buoyant flight. The Common Tern, *Sterna hirundo*, is known by the red bill with a black tip, but can be difficult to distinguish from the Arctic Tern (*S. paradisea*), which has a pure red bill and shorter legs. It is the commoner species in England, though the Arctic Tern predominates in Scotland and Ireland. Other species of tern breeding in Britain differ in bill colour and size. Immatures have a dark leading edge to the wing and brown scaly patterning on the back.

Like all terns, this is a summer visitor to Britain. Its principal wintering areas are off the west coast of Africa, but it is out-classed as a traveller by the Arctic Tern, which winters in Antarctic waters. It nests colonially, laying 2 or 3 eggs in a simple scrape on sand or shingle. The chicks stay close to the nest at first, and can fly after 4 weeks.

Common Tern settling on eggs

Puffins and burrows

Puffin

Length 12 inches (31 cm)

With pied breeding plumage and a huge, vividly coloured bill, the Puffin, *Fratercula arctica*, can hardly be mistaken for anything else. In winter the bill is duller and the horny triangle above the eye is shed, but the bird retains its distinctive profile. Only juveniles, with their much narrower bills, might cause confusion, but their pale faces bordered by a black collar distinguish them from related seabirds. The flight is swift, usually low over the sea, with rapid beats of the narrow wings.

Puffins dive for their prey of sand eels and other small fish. They are able to catch additional fish while still grasping others, and may turn up at their nest sites holding 6 or more crosswise in the bill (see photograph). They are colonial breeders, nesting in burrows in cliff top turf, either excavated or taken over from rabbits or shearwaters. A single egg is laid, and the chick remains in the burrow for about 7 weeks, for the last 9 days of which it is abandoned by its parents.

Puffin

Wood Pigeon young on nest

Wood Pigeon

Length 16 inches (41 cm)

Larger than the feral town pigeons with which it is often seen feeding, the Wood Pigeon, *Columba palumbus*, is known by the white patch on the neck, and the white bar on the wings, conspicuous in flight. Other identification features are the loud wing claps as it takes off, and the song, a rhythmic sequence of 5 coos, usually repeated 3 times.

In towns, Wood Pigeons may be extremely tame, but in the countryside they are shot as pests, and become wary and vigilant. Unlike some supposed bird pests, the damage they can do to crops is real enough, and their numbers remain large despite shooting. Breeding can take place any time from March to October, and two or more broods may be raised, although only two eggs are laid in any one nest. The latter is a simple platform of twigs placed in a bush or tree; evergreens are preferred early in the year, deciduous trees later. The young are fed on a special secretion from the adult's stomach, and take about a month to fledge.

58

Wood Pigeon

Collared Dove

Collared Dove

Length 12 inches (30 cm)

Smaller size and slimmer build alone should distinguish *Streptopelia decaocto* from the Wood Pigeon. The narrow black half-collar is an additional recognition point. Confusion is more likely with the similarly sized Turtle Dove (*S. turtur*); however, the latter has black and rufous mottled upperparts, whereas those of the Collared Dove are a uniform warm grey. In flight, the tail appears square-ended, with the base black and the rest white as seen from below. The Turtle Dove has a more rounded tail, with a less extensive white tip. The song of the Collared Dove is a repetition of 3 coos, with the emphasis on the second.

So familiar is this bird today, that it is hard to realise that it was unknown in Britain before 1955. Its colonisation of this country followed a spectacular spread across Europe from the 1930's onward, starting from a centre in the Balkans. It can breed almost any time between February and November. Two eggs are laid and two broods usually raised.

Collared Dove nest and eggs

Cuckoo

Cuckoo

Length 13 inches (33 cm)

The song of the Cuckoo, *Cuculus canorus*, may well be the best-known of all bird sounds, yet many people remain vague about the bird's appearance. Often seen in flight, its shallow wing beats and pointed head silhouette are features which distinguish it. Seen at rest, the Cuckoo's barred underparts and grey upperparts are reminiscent of a Sparrowhawk, but its bill shape, white spotted tail and much shorter legs should prevent confusion. Young birds have a white spot on the back of the head, and some of them have predominantly rufous plumage, increasing the resemblance to a Kestrel. As well as the familiar 'cuckoo', there are a variety of bubbling and chuckling calls.

Cuckoos are brood parasites, laying their eggs in the nests of other birds. From 6 to 18 eggs may be laid by a single female, though only one per nest. Each female specialises in one particular host species, common victims in Britain being the Reed Warbler, Meadow Pipit and Dunnock.

Young Cuckoo being fed by reed warbler

Tawny Owl young in nest box

Tawny Owl

Length 15 inches (38 cm)

Mottled brown or rufous upperparts, heavily streaked underparts and large size identify the Tawny Owl, *Strix aluco*, when a good view is obtained. Like the much paler Barn Owl (see page 66), it has dark eyes; all other British Owls have yellow or orange eyes. As it is a highly nocturnal species, such views are only likely when a roosting bird is spotted, usually huddled against a tree trunk, or in ivy. At night, the best means of identification are its calls – its quavering hoot, or a sharp 'kewick'.

Chiefly a woodland Owl, the Tawny Owl also occurs on farmland and in towns. Rather than quartering the ground in flight like the Barn Owl, it prefers to sit and wait for prey. Breeding is much affected by fluctuations in rodent numbers. Tree cavities are the commonest nest sites, but Tawny Owls will readily accept specially designed nest boxes, as illustrated. 2 to 5 eggs are laid, and the young fledge in about 5 weeks.

Tawny Owl

Barn Owl nest and eggs

Barn Owl

Length 13–14 inches (33–36 cm)

Seen unexpectedly at dusk, the Barn Owl, *Tyto alba*, gives an impression of complete ghostly whiteness. A better view by daylight shows that the upperparts are in fact pale sandy buff. A further distinctive feature is the heart-shaped face outline, in contrast to the circular one of other owls. Sometimes seen patrolling a field in broad daylight, the Barn Owl's buoyant moth-like flight is characteristic; only the Short-eared Owl (*Asio flammeus*), an altogether darker bird, behaves similarly.

Unhappily, the Barn Owl is decreasing seriously in many areas. Loss of habitat and high mortality through road casualties have all played a part. Elms, now gravely depleted by disease, provided many of the large tree cavities used for nesting, From 3 to 7 or more eggs are laid, depending on rodent numbers, and the young stay in the nest for up to 12 weeks. Their presence is often betrayed by their loud snoring hisses. In a good year, Barn Owls may have two broods.

Barn Owl

Swift at nest

Swift

Length 6½ inches (16 cm)

Sickle-shaped wings and dark colouration both above and below distinguish the Swift, *Apus apus*, from the Swallows and Martins (see pages 78–80) with which it is sometimes confused. Its high-speed flight and frequently-uttered shrill screaming calls are also recognition features.

Swifts are the most aerial of all birds, even sleeping and mating on the wing. They land only at the nest site, and show an amazing ability to fly straight into tiny openings apparently at full speed. The nest itself is a collection of straws and feathers gathered in flight and cemented together with saliva. 2 or 3 eggs are laid in early May, soon after the birds return from their winter quarters in central Africa. The fledging period of the young ranges from 5 to 8 weeks because they are able to survive when bad weather interrupts their parents' foraging by becoming torpid. Development then ceases for a time. Swifts do not breed until they are 3 years old, so the intervening period is spent virtually continuously on the wing.

Swift in flight

Kingfisher nestlings

Kingfisher

Length 6½ inches (16 cm)

The vivid colouring of *Alcedo atthis* permits instant identification. Surprisingly though, this bird is often inconspicuous in its natural habitat, perched on a shaded riverside branch or post. Its dumpy, large-headed silhouette and long dagger of a bill may then be better clues than colour. When it flies, however, there is no missing its brilliant blue back and rump and whirring wing-beats. Young birds are as brightly coloured as adults.

Kingfishers usually watch for prey from a perch, but sometimes hover. A swift plunge secures the small fish it sights, which is then taken back to the perch and beaten to kill it, before being swallowed head first. For nesting, a tunnel is excavated in a river bank, and 7 eggs are laid in a chamber at the end. This quickly becomes fouled with fish remains, so for protection the young retain sheaths around the developing feathers for a long time. This gives them a strange spiky appearance as shown in the photograph. Kingfishers are resident in Britain.

70

Kingfisher with stickleback just caught

Green Woodpecker and nest hole

Green Woodpecker
Length 12½ inches (32 cm)
Seen at close range, the striking colouration of the Green Woodpecker, *Picus viridis*, makes identification easy. It is even possible to distinguish the bird's sex, as males have a red moustache streak, females a black one. The call is also distinctive – a loud, ringing series of notes resembling wild laughter. The flight is strongly undulating like that of all woodpeckers, but the head and neck are longer than the Great Spotted Woodpecker's.

Although primarily a woodland bird, the Green Woodpecker may also be seen on farmland or in gardens. As well as finding insects in tree bark like other woodpeckers, it also lands on flat ground, including lawns, to feed off ants, which are taken from their burrows by means of the extraordinarily long tongue. The nest is a deep chamber excavated in a tree trunk in which 5 to 7 white eggs are laid. Young Green Woodpeckers in juvenile plumage have scaly barring on the underparts, and lack the facial markings of the adults, although they do have red crowns.

Green Woodpecker

Great spotted Woodpecker fledgling

Great Spotted Woodpecker
Length 9 inches (23 cm)
Dendrocopos major is smaller than the Green Woodpecker, and has totally different colouring. Care must also be taken to distinguish it from the scarcer Lesser Spotted Woodpecker (*Dendrocopos minor*). The latter is not only smaller, but has a strongly barred back. In spring, the Great Spotted Woodpecker can often be located by its 'drumming' – a loud echoing rattle made by rapid blows of the bill against a branch. The male can be distinguished by his red nape patch.

The drumming action should not be confused with nest excavation. This is carried out with slow, deliberate but very powerful blows to produce a chamber similar to the Green Woodpecker's but smaller. Well-grown young are extremely noisy, and often draw attention to the nest with their hunger calls. This is one of the few birds in which juveniles are brighter than adults, having complete red crown patches which the adults lack.

74

Great spotted Woodpecker at nest hole

Skylark

Skylark

Length 7 inches (18 cm)

The Skylark, *Alauda arvensis*, is famed for its aerial song, but on the ground it is a rather nondescript bird. In the open grassy areas it frequents, the Meadow Pipit is the species with which confusion is likely. However, the Skylark is a good deal larger and stouter, with a much shorter tail and a slight crest. In flight, it shows white outer tail feathers like a Pipit, but it also has a conspicuous whitish border along the hind edge of the wing. The song is remarkable for its length – a varied cascade of notes which may continue for some minutes as the bird dances and hovers several hundred feet up.

Skylarks feed on the ground, taking a variety of insects and seeds. The nest is a simple grass cup placed in a hollow, and 3 to 5 eggs are laid. The young leave the nest only 9 days after hatching, very early for a small song bird. Thereafter they depend on ground cover and their own excellent camouflage for protection until they are able to fly when 20 days old.

Skylark nest and eggs

Swallow nest and eggs

Swallow

Length 7–8 inches (18–20 cm)

Despite the reputation as a symbol of summer, many people confuse the Swallow, *Hirundo rustica*, with the House Martin, *Delichon urbica* (see page 80), although the two species are quite easy to distinguish. The Swallow has completely dark upperparts, buff underparts with a chestnut throat, and much longer tail streamers. House Martins are known by their conspicuous white rump patch, white underparts and shorter forked tail.

Swallows feed on aerial insects, captured in flight, and often swoop low over water to drink in flight. British breeding Swallows are among the greatest travellers, wintering in Cape Province, South Africa. Despite this huge journey, adults often return annually to the same breeding site, although year-old birds must find a new one. The nest is typically on a beam in an open building such as a barn, shed or even garage. 4 to 6 eggs are laid, and 2 or 3 broods may be reared during the course of a summer.

78

Swallow at nest

House Martin juvenile

House Martin

Length 5 inches (13 cm)

Plumage differences between this species, *Delichon urbica*, and the Swallow have been explained on the previous page. A further distinction is provided by their nests.

Both species make a nest of mud with grass or straw strengthening and a feather lining; however, that of the Swallow is open above, while the House Martin's abuts onto an eave or ledge above, leaving only a narrow entrance hole. Consequently, House Martin nests are always on the outside of a building, never inside as with the Swallow's. Another difference is that Swallows are solitary nesters, whereas House Martins are colonial, their nests often touching each other. Colonies on cliffs, the original natural site, occur in places. 2 or 3 broods are reared each year, and young from an early brood may help feed those of a later one. As a result, a large House Martin colony often presents an appearance of intense activity with swarms of birds swooping in and out with excited chirruping.

80

House Martin

Meadow Pipit

Meadow Pipit

Length 5½ inches (14 cm)

Differences from the Skylark have been described under that species (see page 76), but the Meadow Pipit, *Anthus pratensis*, also needs to be distinguished from the very similar Tree Pipit (*A. trivialis*). This bird prefers open woodland, but can overlap with the Meadow Pipit in some habitats. Seen together, the Tree Pipit appears somewhat larger and brighter, but the best distinction is its pink, rather than brown legs.

Pipits also make aerial song flights, but not nearly so extended as the Skylark's. The Meadow Pipit rises from the ground to about 100 feet, then planes down on set wings. As it rises it utters an accelerating series of simple notes which slow down again as it descends. Meadow Pipits occur in a variety of open habitats from grasslands to quite high moorlands, where they are often the commonest bird. The nest is a cup of grass stems concealed in a grass or heather tussock, and 4 or 5 eggs are usual.

Meadow Pipit nest and eggs

Pied Wagtail nest and eggs

Pied Wagtail

Length 7 inches (18 cm)

Striking black and white plumage and a long tail, constantly wagged up and down, make an adult Pied Wagtail, *Motacilla alba*, easy to recognise. The duller, slightly yellow-tinged juveniles could be puzzling, but there are usually adults in close attendance. As with all wagtails, the flight of this bird is strongly undulating.

Although commonest in waterside habitats, the Pied Wagtail may also be seen around farms, or in town parks and gardens. It is fond of foraging on roads underneath trees for insects that have fallen off the foliage. Sewage farms are a particularly favoured habitat. The nest is a substantial cup of grass, lined with hair and placed in some kind of cavity, either a natural one in a bank, or very often one in a building or other man-made structure. 5 or 6 grey speckled eggs are laid, and there are two broods. During winter, Pied Wagtails often gather at dusk in large communal roosts on well-heated buildings, such as factories and hospitals.

Pied Wagtail

Wren

Wren

Length 4 inches (10 cm)

An explosive burst of song from a garden shrub may be the first sign of this common but skulking little bird. Seen in the open, the small size, short upward-pointing tail, and barred brown plumage of the Wren, *Troglodytes troglodytes*, are unmistakable; it only seems amazing that so loud a voice could emanate from so tiny a bird. Its flight is whirring and direct, and its movements busy and restless as it seeks small insects in low bushes and ground cover. Wrens scold intruders with sharp ticking notes when nest or young are threatened.

Wrens occur in many different habitats. They are actually more abundant than generally realised, but their numbers can drop sharply following a hard winter. The domed nest is concealed in some recess in a tree trunk or bank, or in a variety of bizarre sites in and around buildings and gardens. Several unlined nests are made in addition to that used for nesting. 5 or 6 eggs are laid and there are two broods.

Wren at nest

Blackcap nest and eggs

Blackcap

Length 5½ inches (14 cm)

Only the male Blackcap (*Sylvia atricapilla*) deserves its name, as the female has a reddish brown cap. Unless the cap can be seen, it is difficult to distinguish the Blackcap from the very plainly clad Garden Warbler (*S. borin*). Blackcaps are commoner in woods and gardens, Garden Warblers in scrubby areas, but the two species occur together in many places. Song is some guide, as with practice, the Blackcap's warbling can be differentiated as richer, but less sustained.

The Blackcap's nest is also very similar to that of the Garden Warbler; it tends to be placed higher, and more often includes moss, but sight of the bird is the only sure means of identification. 4 to 6 eggs are laid, and there may be two broods in southern England. In autumn, the diet changes from insects to berries, to gain fuel for migration. Most Blackcaps travel south in winter, but a few remain here, and may be seen at garden bird-tables in hard weather.

Blackcap male and young

Dunnock

Dunnock

Length 6 inches (15 cm)

Plain grey head and underparts with streaked brown back and flanks distinguish the Dunnock, *Prunella modularis*, from other 'small brown birds'. The plumage is quite Sparrow-like, but this species is easily told from Sparrows by its much finer bill. At close range, adults show a striking brick-red eye colour. At longer distances, another useful recognition feature is the incessant fidgeting movements of the wings. The song is rather reminiscent of the Wren's, but lacks the final trill with which the latter ends.

Dunnocks feed on small insects and seeds. The nest is a well-made grassy cup lined with moss, concealed in a dense bush or bramble. 4 or 5 deep blue eggs are laid, and there are 2 or 3 broods. Dunnocks have a complex mating system in which polygamy and changes of partner are not uncommon. British Dunnocks are extremely sedentary, though continental birds are more mobile.

Dunnock nest and eggs

Robin nest and eggs

Robin

Length 5½ inches (14 cm)

No bird could be more familiar than the Robin, *Erithacus rubecula*, Britain's favourite and the symbol of Christmas. However, the juveniles, with their spotted yellow-ochre underparts, often go unidentified. In any case, the portly outline of the Robin, with head sunk into the back, is an easy one to recognise.

Robins are strongly territorial and pugnacious, and will react aggressively to even a tuft of red feathers, placed within their domain. During the breeding season, a pair holds a joint territory, but territories continue during the winter as well, with males and females defending separate areas. Robins make substantial nests which are usually skilfully concealed in a bank or ivy-covered tree trunk, but all kinds of human buildings and artefacts are used, including sheds, garages, old kettles and so on. Open-fronted nestboxes are readily accepted. 5 or 6 eggs are laid, and 2, sometimes 3 broods are raised in a year.

Robin

Nightingale nest and eggs

Nightingale

Length 6½ inches (16 cm)

Despite its fame as a songster, relatively few people would be able to recognise the Nightingale, *Luscinia megarhynchos*, if they saw it. Plain brown above and off-white below, the Nightingale's most striking field character is its rich rufous tail. This feature is often the last thing to be seen as the bird dives into a thicket, for it is a shy and retiring species. When it is seen well, the resemblance in shape to its close relative the Robin is noticeable, though it is not quite so dumpy in build. Its song is most often confused with that of the Blackcap's. However, the real thing is much more powerful and varied, and identified by a series of long-drawn notes ending in a rich chuckle. Moreover, it really is uttered at night as well as day.

Nightingales are summer visitors, and rear only a single brood during their stay here. The nest is a cup of grass on a foundation of oak leaves, skilfully hidden on the ground amongst nettles or in low undergrowth, and 4 to 6 eggs are laid.

Nightingale feeding young

Blackbird nest and eggs

Blackbird

Length 10 inches (25 cm)

Whether it is the jet black male with yellow bill, or the browner, dark-billed female, most people would recognise the Blackbird, *Turdus merula*, in the garden. Young birds are paler below, with dark spotting, and could be confused with other thrushes, but they are always much darker above. Immature males in autumn, moulting into their black adult plumage, often present a curious patchwork of black and brown. A few white feathers somewhere in the plumage are not uncommon, and occasional individuals are nearly completely white.

Originally a woodland bird, the Blackbird is also common on farmland and in towns. The nest is usually placed a few feet up in a bush, or on a ledge of a building. It is a mud-reinforced grass structure, with a grassy lining. 3 to 5 eggs are laid, and 3 or even more broods may be reared in a year. In winter, our Blackbird population is swelled by migrants from Northern Europe.

Blackbird

Song Thrush nest and eggs

Song Thrush

Length 9 inches (23 cm)

Turdus philomelos is a rather small thrush with plain olive-brown upper-parts, and a yellow-ochre, black-spotted breast. It is distinguished from the Mistle Thrush by size, more restricted spotting on the underparts, and uniform tail colour. Young birds resemble adults. Like all thrushes, it has a rich and melodious song, but it is easily distinguished from the Blackbird and Mistle Thrush by its habit of repeating phrases several times in succession.

A distinctive feeding technique used by this species is its use of a convenient stone as an 'anvil' on which to crack open the shells of snails, a habit which endears it to gardeners! The nest, placed in similar situations to the Blackbird's is at once known by its smooth mud lining. The 3 to 5 eggs are equally distinctive, with their bright blue colour and black spots. Many nests fall to predators, but the birds persist to rear 2 or 3 broods a year. Some Song Thrushes migrate south during winter.

Song Thrush

Redwing and young

Redwing

Length 8½ inches (22 cm)

This small thrush, *Turdus iliacus*, might be confused with the Song Thrush but can easily be identified by its conspicuous white eyebrow, and by a bright rufous patch on the flanks and underwing, easily discerned in flight. It is a highly gregarious species in winter, whereas the Song Thrush remains solitary. It is often seen in mixed flocks with Fieldfares. Migrants passing over at night reveal themselves with 'seeep' flight calls.

Like the Fieldfare, this is principally a winter visitor, though some have become established as breeding birds in Scotland and northern England. When hard weather brings it into our gardens, favourite foods are *Pyracantha* and *Cotoneaster* berries, as seen in the illustration. Breeding birds may form small colonies, and nests are sited at moderate height in bushes or tree forks. The nest is lined with grass, unlike that of the Song Thrush, and the 5 or 6 eggs resemble small versions of the Blackbird's.

Redwing in snow

Mistle Thrush nest and eggs

Mistle Thrush
Length 10½ inches (27 cm)
Largest of our thrushes, the Mistle Thrush, *Turdus viscivorus*, has white underparts with bold black spotting continued well down along flanks and belly. The tail shows white-tipped outer feathers. Overhead, it reveals conspicuous white wing linings like the Fieldfare, though the uniform brown upperparts prevent confusion with that species. Its song resembles the Blackbird's, but is shorter and more strident, often delivered from a treetop in the teeth of a gale, earning it the country name of 'stormcock'. The alarm call sounds like a football supporter's rattle.

The Mistle Thrush nests early, sometimes starting at the end of February. The nest is placed in a tree, often quite high. It resembles the Blackbird's, but more moss is used. Pieces of rubbish, such as plastic or baling twine are often woven into the rim. 3 to 5 eggs are laid and there are two broods.

Mistle Thrush

Sedge Warbler nest and eggs

Sedge Warbler

Length 5 inches (13 cm)

Closely related to the Reed Warbler (*A. scirpaceus*) which is illustrated with the Cuckoo, the Sedge Warbler, *Acrocephalus schoenobaenus*, is distinguished by its streaked upperparts. The crown is dark, contrasting with a strong white eye-stripe. Both species have loud grating, chattering songs, but whereas the Reed Warbler repeats phrases, the Sedge Warbler's is more continuous and varied, and often includes mimicry of other birds.

Sedge Warblers arrive in May, and occupy a wide variety of marshy habitats and even some drier scrubby areas. The nest is sometimes woven round plant stems like a Reed Warbler's, but may just be placed in a low fork or bramble. 5 or 6 eggs are laid, and two broods may be reared in southern England. Prior to their southward migration, Sedge Warblers may almost double their weight with fat as fuel for the long journey to Africa south of the Sahara. Some are capable of managing this in one long flight, though others make stopovers in the Iberian peninsula.

Sedge Warbler

Common Whitethroat nest and eggs

Whitethroat
Length 5½ inches (14 cm)
As the name suggests, both sexes of this species, *Sylvia communis*, show a conspicuous white throat, contrasting with the pinkish brown underparts. There is a bright tawny area on the wing, and the slightly crested head is grey in the male, brownish in the female. White outer tail feathers are noticeable in flight. The smaller Lesser Whitethroat, (*S. curruca*), is a greyer bird with a dark patch through the eye. Alarm calls are harsh, and there is a chattering song often delivered in a dancing display flight.

Whitethroats are the typical Warbler of roadside verges, hedgerows and scrub, but they are less numerous than formerly, having been badly affected by drought conditions in the African wintering areas. Fortunately, there has recently been some recovery. The frail, neat nest of stems and rootlets is usually sited on a bramble or other stem within a patch of nettles. 4 or 5 eggs are laid, and two broods reared during the summer.

Common Whitethroat

Dipper nest

Dipper

Length 7 inches (18 cm)

Plump-bodied, with a short tail and distinctive plumage, appearance would be enough to identify the Dipper, *Cinclus cinclus*. Its ability to walk under water, and its habit of bobbing on a rock in midstream, also make identification very simple.

Rushing mountain streams are the Dipper's home, and it patrols these in its search for aquatic insects, rarely being seen away from the water. As well as walking on the bottom, it also swims well. Its nest is large for the size of the bird, a domed structure of grass and moss placed in a cleft in the river bank, or under a bridge. A common site is behind a waterfall, the curtain of water presenting no barrier to the Dipper. The 4 to 6 white eggs may be laid as early as the beginning of March. Young Dippers spend up to 25 days in the nest after hatching; this is long for a bird of this size, but it is essential that they be fully developed to cope immediately with their turbulent environment.

Dipper

Willow Warbler nest and eggs

Willow Warbler

Length 4½ inches (11 cm)

One of our commonest summer visitors, the Willow Warbler, *Phylloscopus trochilus*, can easily be confused with its close relative the Chiffchaff (*P. collybita*). Both are small, slim warblers, olive above and yellowish on the breast, with distinct pale eye-stripes. The Willow Warbler is on the whole brighter and yellower, and its legs are fairly pale; the Chiffchaff is a greyer bird with dark legs. Song is the easiest guide however. The Willow Warbler delivers a sweet, descending trickle of notes, while the Chiffchaff says its name – a repeated 'chiff-chaff-chiff-chaff' sustained for several seconds and alternating with a very quiet grating call.

Willow Warblers arrive early in spring, and nest building starts before the end of April. The nest, a beautiful domed structure of grass lined with feathers, is cleverly concealed on the ground under a grass tussock, dead bracken, etc. The Chiffchaff's is similar, but placed a foot or two off the ground. 5 or 6 eggs are laid, and usually only one brood is reared.

Willow Warbler and young

Goldcrest nest and eggs

Goldcrest

Length 3½ inches (9 cm)

Size alone would identify the Goldcrest, *Regulus regulus*, our smallest bird, were it not for its scarcer relative the Firecrest (*R. ignicapilla*). Both are greenish above and off-white below, and have colourful crown stripes, but the Firecrest additionally has a black and white eye-stripe and a golden patch on the sides of the neck. In the Goldcrest, females have a pure yellow crown stripe, while the male's has an orange centre. The Goldcrest's song is a series of very high-pitched notes ending in a short flourish which is lacking in the Firecrest's version.

Goldcrests frequent coniferous habitats, not only woodland, but suburban areas with firs and cedars, and yew-filled churchyards. The nest is a beautiful structure of moss and spider's silk, lined with feathers, and suspended beneath the branch of a conifer at almost any height from 3 to 40 feet. 5 to 8 tiny buff eggs are laid. After hatching, the young spend up to 3 weeks in the nest, a long time for so small a bird.

Goldcrest at nest

Spotted Flycatcher nest and eggs

Spotted Flycatcher
Length 5½ inches (14 cm)
Perched very upright on a fence, a greyish-brown little bird suddenly takes to the air in swift flight, adroitly seizes a passing insect and returns to its perch. This piece of behaviour alone is sufficient to identify it as a Spotted Flycatcher, *Muscicapa striata*. A closer view shows a streaked breast and a slightly crested crown, but the name Spotted really applies to the juveniles, which have dark spots below and pale ones above.

Spotted Flycatchers like areas with mature trees in the vicinity of buildings. Parks, or the grounds of churches or stately homes are ideal, but they occur in many suburban areas as well. Late arrivals in spring, they start nesting at once, choosing a ledge on a building or tree, or creeper on a wall. Open-fronted nestboxes are also favoured. The nest is a compact cup of grass and moss, with hair and feathers in the lining, and 4 or 5 eggs are laid. Usually only one brood is reared.

Spotted Flycatcher at nest

Long-tailed Tit

Long-tailed Tit
Length 5½ inches (14 cm)
Were it not for its very long tail, *Aegithalos caudatus* would be our second smallest bird. Size, shape and the beautiful pink, black and white plumage make it unmistakable, as does its habit of moving about in noisy restless parties.

The Long-tailed Tit is famous for its beautiful nest, the most elaborate of any British bird. It is composed chiefly of moss and lichen bound together with spiders' webs, and lined with hundreds of feathers. It is a domed nest shaped like an upright rugby ball, with a small round entrance near the top. Many nests are placed a few feet up in some thorny bush, gorse being a favourite, but others are sited quite high in a tree, skilfully blended into a fork to conceal the outline. Seven to twelve eggs are laid, and there is only one brood. Outside the breeding season Long-tailed Tits wander through all kinds of hedgerows and scrub, and a few visit gardens. They suffer considerably in hard winters.

Long-tailed Tit nest

Coal Tit nest and eggs

Coal Tit

Length 4½ inches (11 cm)

Smaller than the Blue Tit, the Coal Tit, *Parus ater*, is at once known by the black cap with prominent white nape patch, and by the two whitish wing-bars. Two somewhat similar species are the Marsh and Willow Tits (*P. palustris* and *P. montanus*), but these have plain black caps without the white nape, and they lack wing bars.

Coal Tits are particularly fond of coniferous woodland, where their fine bills are suited to extracting insects from among pine needles. However, they are also seen in other habitats including gardens. The nest is built inside a hole like that of other tits, but is quite often at ground level in a bank or stump; old rodent holes are a common choice. Nest boxes are taken, but less regularly than by the other tits. 7 to 11 eggs are laid, and as with all tits, only a single brood is normally reared.

Coal Tit

Blue Tit

Length 4½ inches (11 cm)

Next to the Robin, the Blue Tit, *Parus caeruleus* is probably our best-loved garden bird, and its blue and yellow plumage with black and white head markings make it easy to recognise. Juveniles are duller, lacking the blue crowns of their parents, but are still easily recognised by their small compact shape and acrobatic feeding behaviour.

Principally a bird of oak woodland during the breeding season, Blue Tits will also breed in gardens where nest boxes are provided. Their nest-building can be watched from late winter onwards, and egg-laying may start at the beginning of April. As there may be up to 16 eggs to be laid, one a day before incubation commences, the breeding cycle is prolonged, and the noisy parties of juveniles may not emerge until June or July. Blue Tits visit nest boxes with astounding frequency, delivering small caterpillars or other insects. They are notorious for their ability to peck open milk bottle tops.

Blue Tit feeding

Great Tit nest and eggs

Great Tit
Length 5½ inches (14 cm)
Another popular garden bird, though not quite as numerous as the Blue Tit, the Great Tit, *Parus major*, is known by its large size, black cap and black band down the belly. The latter is much broader in males, enabling the sexes to be told apart fairly easily. White outer tail feathers are another distinctive feature. The song of the Great Tit, a cheery 'tee-cher, tee-cher' is a typical sound of early spring.

Like the preceding species, this is primarily a woodland bird which has learned to exploit gardens for food in winter, and has been encouraged to nest in them by the provision of nest boxes. Pleased as we may be to see them there, gardens rarely provide the same spring abundance of insects as an oakwood, so the broods reared in gardens are smaller in average number. The nest, similar to the Blue Tit's, is made of moss and grass, lined with hair and a few feathers. Clutch size ranges from 5 to 12 and a single brood is raised.

Great Tit at nest hole

Nuthatch nest and eggs

Nuthatch
Length 5½ inches (14 cm)
No other bird habitually walks down a tree-trunk head first. This habit alone would identify the Nuthatch, *Sitta europaea*, even without its unusual shape and plumage. It is a stocky bird with short legs and tail, but with a long dagger-like bill, slightly up-tilted. The upperparts are grey with a black stripe through the eye, the flanks and belly are reddish brown, and there are white spots either side of the tail tip. In flight it shows a pale wing bar. It has a variety of loud whistles and trilling calls.

It owes its name to its ability to open nuts and acorns by wedging them in a crevice and hammering them with its robust bill. Holes in trees are the usual nest site though nest boxes are sometimes taken, and the entrance hole is plastered with mud to reduce it to exactly the right size. The 6 to 9 eggs are laid on a bed of bark flakes; no other material is used. There is only one brood.

Nuthatch at nest hole

Treecreeper nest and eggs

Treecreeper
Length 5 inches (13 cm)
Moving spirally up a tree-trunk in short hops, using its stiff tail as a prop, the Treecreeper, *Certhia familiaris*, is easily recognised. A good view reveals that its brown upperparts are intricately patterned with streaks and bars to help it blend with bark, and it has a fine, down-curved bill with which it probes into cracks for tiny insects. When it flies, it reveals a pale tawny wing bar.

Treecreepers normally build a nest behind loose bark, though they can sometimes be tempted into nestboxes specially designed to simulate a narrow crevice. Occasionally sheds in woodland, noticeboards, etc. provide sites. The nest consists of a foundation of twigs supporting a cup of finer material, and 5 or 6 eggs are laid. Two broods are occasionally raised. In winter, Treecreepers venture into hedgerows, gardens and orchards, sometimes mixing with parties of tits.

Treecreeper feeding

Jay nest and eggs

Jay

Length 13½ inches (34 cm)

A piercing harsh screech is often the first clue to the presence of this brightly-coloured but shy bird, *Garrulus glandarius*. Seen properly, its salmon pink plumage, blue barred wings and crest are unmistakable. A more common view, as it flies off in alarm, reveals a conspicuous white rump and wing patches. Seen flying out in the open, the flight appears undulating and rather weak.

Jays eat a variety of plant and animal foods, but acorns are of special importance. The birds bury these in large numbers during autumn, for use later in the winter; as many undoubtedly get missed, Jays are a valuable agent in dispersing oak trees. Normally sedentary, Jays may undertake long journeys when the acorn crop fails. The nest is a frail platform of twigs lined with a cup of rootlets, placed in a tree fork, or creeper such as honeysuckle. 5 or 6 eggs are laid, bearing a close resemblance to the Blackbird's. One brood is reared.

Jay

Magpie nest and eggs

Magpie

Length 18 inches (46 cm)

Familiar and unmistakable, the pied plumage of the Magpie, *Pica pica*, permits instant recognition. Even silhouetted against the light, the exceptionally long tail identifies it. Overhead, the wings appear broad and rounded, and the flight action rather moth-like. The call is a harsh chatter.

Magpies have increased in numbers this century, apparently by learning to utilise suburban habitats as well as rural ones. Since they have a reputation as egg thieves, concern is sometimes expressed that this increase will have an adverse effect on other birds, though in fact eggs form only a small proportion of their very varied diet. The Magpie's own nest would defy most predators: it has an impregnable dome of thorns, and is usually sited in a thorny bush or tree. 5 to 7 eggs are laid, sometimes starting in early March, and a single brood is raised per year. Magpies roost socially, and also form noisy, excited gatherings at times just before the breeding season.

Magpie

Jackdaw nest and eggs

Jackdaw

Length 13 inches (33 cm)

Small size, a pale grey nape contrasting with an otherwise all-black plumage, and a strikingly pale eye distinguishes the Jackdaw, *Corvus monedula*, from the Crow and Rook. It is often found in mixed flocks with Rooks, and its sharp calls of 'kyak' stand out in contrast to the harsh caws of the larger species.

Unlike other Crows, the Jackdaw always nests in a hole of some kind, either a natural one in a cliff or tree, or in some kind of man-made site such as a chimney. The next itself varies greatly in size, according to the space that has to be filled. A small cavity may have a mere lining of wool and grass, while a spacious one may contain a vast foundation of sticks. Where nest sites are plentiful enough, Jackdaws breed colonially. 4 to 6 eggs are laid, and the young remain in the nest for over a month from hatching. Although generally sedentary, Jackdaws may at times wander widely, and there have been several recent records from North America.

Jackdaw

Rookery

Rook

Length 18 inches (46 cm)

Rooks and Crows are frequently confused, although it is usually easy to distinguish them. The most obvious field character of the Rook, *Corvus frugilegus*, is the bare whitish skin on the face and base of the bill. The head outline is also different, with a more pointed bill and higher forehead than the Crow. This is helpful in identifying young Rooks, which have all black faces. An additional characteristic is the 'baggy-trousered' appearance created by loose feathers on the thighs. The call is also much harsher than the Crow's.

Rooks are highly sociable birds, in sharp contrast with Crows. They feed in large flocks on farmland and roost communally. Rookeries are generally situated high up in the smaller branches at the very tops of trees. Breeding starts early in the year, before leaves have emerged, making the birds and their nests highly conspicuous. 3 to 6 eggs are laid and the young fledge about a month after hatching.

Rook

Carrion Crow nest and eggs

Crow

Length 18½ inches (47 cm)

Differences between the Crow, *Corvus corone*, and the Rook have already been explained (see page 134), but in mountainous districts there could be confusion with the much less numerous Raven (*C. corax*). This is a considerably larger bird with a wedge-shaped tail, massive bill and a deep, throaty call. The distinction is much easier in the Highlands of Scotland, as Crows there are 'Hooded': the body is grey, contrasting with the black head, wings and tail.

Crows are solitary, wily birds, scavenging or predating a wide range of foods. They are unpopular with farmers and gamekeepers, and much persecuted, yet they remain common, and have even colonised urban areas. The nest is built in a tree, usually high up, but sometimes in quite low bushes, and also on rock ledges in mountain areas. 3 to 6 eggs are laid, and the young fledge in 4 to 5 weeks. Old Crows' nests last a long time, and provide nest sites for various birds of prey in future years.

Carrion Crow

Starling

Starling nest and eggs

Length 8½ inches (22 cm)

Starlings foraging on a lawn are sometimes confused with Blackbirds, but they are in reality very different birds. The Starling, *Sturnus vulgaris*, is at once known by its glossy, spangled plumage, short tail and the fact that it walks or runs instead of hopping. Juveniles are dull brown, but are still easily recognised by shape and behaviour. In flight, Starlings move swiftly and directly, and generally in at least small parties. At favoured feeding places and still more at their winter roosts, they may swirl about in vast flocks of many thousands.

Always ready to exploit man's activities, the Starling is one of the world's most successful birds. It forages on open ground in many different habitats, prying into the ground for grubs and other insects. The spectacular roosts may be in woods or thickets in the countryside, or on buildings in towns. Starlings nest in cavities, either in trees or buildings, laying 4 to 7 pale blue eggs, and may rear two broods in a favourable year.

Starling

Male House Sparrow

House Sparrow
Length 6 inches (15 cm)
So common that it is often taken for granted, the male House Sparrow, *Passer domesticus*, is actually a handsome bird, with its black, grey and chestnut head markings and white wing bars. Females have similar but duller plumage and plain heads. The less common Tree Sparrow (*P. montanus*) is smaller, with an all chestnut crown and a black spot behind the eye; its sexes are identical. Its call is the familiar, rather monotonous chirp.

Absent only from moorland and extensive woodland, the House Sparrow is one of Britain's most abundant birds. It thrives particularly on farms where cereals are grown, and in towns and gardens where food scraps are fed to the birds. Its untidy domed nest of straw and feathers may be crammed into buildings, dense trees, ivy or haystacks, and breeding activity continues from March to September. 3 to 6 eggs are laid, and there may be up to 4 broods a year.

Female House Sparrow

House Sparrow nest and eggs

Chaffinch nest and eggs

Chaffinch

Length 6 inches (15 cm)

The male Chaffinch (*Fringilla coelebs*) is a colourful bird, with a blue-grey crown, pink underparts and a chestnut back. The female is duller, but either sex is easily recognised by the white shoulder patch and white wing bar, conspicuous in flight. During winter, Chaffinch flocks may mix with those of the closely related Brambling (*F. montifringilla*). This is at once distinguished by having orange instead of white shoulders, and a white rump. The Chaffinch's song is a cheerful descending rattle, ending in a flourish, but its exact form varies greatly from one area to another – one of the best examples of bird song 'dialects'. The alarm call is a loud 'spink'.

Chaffinches are common birds, occurring in woodland, hedgerows, parks and gardens. The nest is a beautiful neat cup of moss and grass, lined with hair and feathers, blended into the fork of a tree or bush so that it is difficult to see. 4 or 5 eggs are laid, and there is one brood. Winter numbers are swelled by the arrival of varying numbers of continental birds.

Male Chaffinch and young

Greenfinch nest and eggs

Greenfinch

Length 6 inches (15 cm)

The male Greenfinch (*Carduelis chloris*) is indeed predominantly green in colour, but the female and the young are duller and brownish, and are occasionally mistaken for House Sparrows. However, there are prominent yellow patches on the wings and tail base in all plumages, so identification should present little difficulty. Flight is undulating, and is often accompanied by a twittering call. The song is a twitter interspersed with a long-drawn wheezy note, and is sometimes delivered in a display flight.

With their robust conical bills, Greenfinches can tackle a variety of seeds, and they are common both on farmland and in parks and gardens. As bird table visitors they are fond of peanuts and sunflower seeds. The nest is a rather untidy cup of grass and moss, lined with hair, rootlets and a few feathers. 4 to 6 eggs are laid, and there are 2 or 3 broods a year. Greenfinches rarely leave Britain, but many make extensive south or south-westerly movements in winter.

Greenfinch

Siskin feeding on peanuts

Siskin

Length 4½ inches (11 cm)

With a black cap, and bright green and yellow plumage, the male Siskin, *Carduelis spinus*, is charming and unmistakable. Females lack the black cap, and are somewhat duller, but are still easily known by the double yellowish wing bar. Only the Greenfinch might be mistaken for a Siskin, but it is considerably larger, and the yellow on its wings is in the form of a patch, rather than bars. When feeding on nut containers, Siskins frequently hang with head down, another identification feature.

Siskins breed in conifer forests, and their main stronghold in Britain is in the Highlands of Scotland. The nest of twigs, grass and moss, lined with softer materials is placed on a conifer branch, often high up. 4 or 5 eggs are laid, and there are two broods. During winter, Siskins typically stay in river valleys with alder trees, but in recent decades have increasingly come into gardens to feed on peanuts. In some winters their numbers are increased by great influxes from northern Europe and Scandinavia.

Siskin

Goldfinch nest and eggs

Goldfinch

Length 5 inches (13 cm)

This species, *Carduelis carduelis*, was once popular as a cage bird. Colourful face markings make the adult distinctive; young birds lack these, but all ages can be recognised by the black and gold wings, especially in flight. The song and calls are a high-pitched twitter.

Goldfinches have the most finely-pointed bills of British finches, and they are ideal for extracting seeds from the heads of such plants as thistles, groundsel and teasels. Consequently, they are most often seen along hedgerows, river banks and waste ground where plants like these occur. Bushes and low trees in hedges, orchards or gardens are the usual nest sites, and the nest itself is a beautiful compact cup lined with white thistle down or wool and a few hairs. 5 or 6 eggs are laid, and there are two or more broods. Many British Goldfinches move to France or Spain in winter.

Goldfinch

Linnet nest and eggs

Linnet

Length 5½ inches (14 cm)

The male Linnet, *Acanthis cannabina*, can be recognised in breeding plumage by its red cap, red breast and chestnut back. Females, juveniles and non-breeding birds lack the red, but can still be identified by the white-edged primary feathers which show as a whitish patch along the edge of the closed wing. Confusion might occur with the Redpoll (*A. flammea*) which also has a pink cap and breast in breeding males. However, the Redpoll is considerably smaller, and has a black bib and forehead, a greyer, streaked back and a double whitish wing bar.

All kinds of small weed seeds form the Linnet's food, and a recent decline in numbers may be linked to the reduction of its food supplies by weed killers. However, it is still common in many heath and hedgerow habitats. The nest is a slightly untidy cup of grass stems lined with hair and wool. Thorny bushes are the usual site, and the nests are sometimes grouped in small colonies. 4 to 6 eggs are laid, and there are 2 or 3 broods.

Linnet and young

Bullfinch nest and eggs

Bullfinch
Length 6 inches (15 cm)
Attired in pink, grey, black and white, the male Bullfinch, *Pyrrhula pyrrhula*, is a beautiful bird. Females are duller, but have essentially the same pattern. Juveniles lack the black cap, but all plumages have a conspicuous white rump patch, contrasting with the black tail. The call is a mellow, piping 'deuu'.

The short, blunt bill is ideally suited for shearing through leaves and buds, and unfortunately, these are all too often those of fruit trees and garden shrubs. Consequently, the bird is regarded as a pest in some areas, and may be controlled by shooting. Its nest is a frail platform of twigs supporting a neat cup of rootlets. It is usually well hidden deep in a bush. 4 to 6 eggs are laid, and there are two broods. It is highly sedentary unlike many finches, rarely moving more than a few kilometres outside the breeding season.

Bullfinch and young

Yellowhammer nest and eggs

Yellowhammer
Length 6½ inches (16 cm)
The male Yellowhammer, *Emberiza citrinella*, is unmistakable with bright yellow head and underparts. Females and young are duller, but all plumages show a conspicuous chestnut rump and white outer tail feathers in flight. The song is a repetition of several short, buzzing notes ending with a long one; it is sometimes rendered 'little bit of bread and no cheese'.

Yellowhammers occur on all types of open ground, including farmland, heaths and young conifer plantations. They feed principally on seeds and other vegetable matter, with a few insects. The nest is a substantial cup of grass, lined with finer material, and is placed in a hollow on a bank, or very low in bush or bramble. 3 or 4 eggs are laid; like those of other buntings, they are marked with irregular fine lines, which has given them the country name of 'scribbling larks'. 2 or 3 broods may be reared. Yellow-hammers form flocks in winter, but British-bred birds do not appear to travel far.

Yellowhammer and young

Reed Bunting nest and eggs

Reed Bunting

Length 6 inches (15 cm)

A jet black head and white collar distinguishes the male Reed Bunting, *Emberiza schoeniclus*, in breeding plumage. This feature is lacking in females and other plumages, but a dark moustache streak is always noticeable. The upperparts are warm brown, streaked with black, and the shoulders chestnut. White outer tail feathers are shown in flight. The commonest call is a thin 'sooeet'.

Typically birds of water-sides or marshy areas, Reed Buntings have expanded their habitat to include drier areas, and now occur in some of the same places as Yellowhammers. Also, they are becoming increasingly common as bird table visitors to gardens in winter. The nest is a cup of grass stems built into the base of a tussock of grass or rushes, and 4 or 5 eggs are laid. When an incubating bird is disturbed it frequently goes off fluttering along the ground as though injured, in order to distract predators from the nest. Two broods are usually reared.

Reed Bunting male and young

INDEX

Other titles in this series:

Butterflies

Mediterranean Wild Flowers

Wild Flowers of Mountain and Moorland

Coastal Wild Flowers

Herbs and Medicinal Plants

Seashells and Seaweeds

Wild Flowers of Roadsides and Waste Places

Weeds

Trees

Mushrooms

Woodland Wild Flowers

Dr Philip Burton is an ornithologist who works for the British Museum (Natural History) at Tring.

Most of the photographs in this book were supplied by Natural Science Photos, and are the work of the following photographers: Les Johnstone p. 1, 45, 47, 87; Peter Ward p. 2; Richard Revels p. 4, 56, 59, 90, 139; Philip Burton p. 5, 10, 26, 44, 50, 63, 77, 91, 92, 98, 106, 110, 122, 128, 130, 152, 156; F. Greenaway p. 6, 8; E. H. Herbert p. 7, 33, 37, 39, 71, 75, 111; Brian Gibbs p. 9; C. Blaney p. 11, 13, 15, 16, 65; Herbert Axell p. 14, 34, 35, 49, 54, 62, 80, 93, 99; A. Winspear Cundall p. 17; Don MacCaskill p. 19, 23 top, 24, 25, 73; Alan Barnes p. 20, 76, 95, 105, 116, 119, 155; Richard Kemp p. 21; C. F. E. Smedley p. 23 bottom; Ian West p. 27, 31, 120, 140, 145; Derick Bonsall p. 29, 41, 57, 82, 103, 109, 113, 115, 123, 125, 143, 151, 153; John Bingley p. 38; J. D. Bakewell p. 43, 85; W. R. Tarboton p. 48; C. A. Walker p. 51, 107, 157; Andrew Watts p. 52; J. Plant p. 53; Geoffrey Kinns p. 55, 129; O. C. Roura p. 58, 121, 147; D. Meredith p. 60; Michael Rose p. 67, 97; P. A. Bowman p. 74; A. Shears p. 89, 127; John Staples p. 131, 133, 137; I. G. Johnson p. 134; A. L. Goodson p. 135; Johan Elzenga p. 141 top; John Mountford p. 149. Photographs kindly supplied by Eric and David Hosking appear on pages 68 (photographer John Hawkins), 69, 72, 81 (John Hawkins), 86, 100, 101 (John Hawkins). All other photographs by Philip Burton.

ELM TREE BOOKS
Published by the Penguin Group
27 Wrights Lane, London W8 5TZ, England
Viking Penguin Inc., 40 West 23rd Street, New York, New York 10010, U.S.A.
Penguin Books Australia Ltd, Ringwood, Victoria, Australia
Penguin Books Canada Ltd, 2801 John Street, Markham, Ontario, Canada L3R 1B4
Penguin Books (N.Z.) Ltd, 182–190 Wairau Road, Auckland 10, New Zealand
Penguin Books Ltd, Registered Offices: Harmondsworth, Middlesex, England
First published in Great Britain 1988 by Elm Tree Books
Copyright © 1988 by Philip Burton
All rights reserved.
ISBN 0-241-12162-0
ISBN 0-241-12161-2 Pbk
Printed and bound in Spain by Cayfosa Industria Gráfica, Barcelona